Successful Children's Parties

Successful Children's Parties

JULIA GOODWIN

WARD LOCK

Acknowledgements

Thanks to Hilary Westlake for her food ideas and to Diana Williamson for typing everything. And, of course, to Anna and Oliver who taught me all I know about children's parties!

A WARD LOCK BOOK

This edition published in the UK 1995 by Ward Lock
Wellington House, 125 Strand, LONDON WC2R OBB

A Cassell Imprint

Distributed in the United States by Sterling Publishing Co., Inc.
387 Park Avenue South, New York, NY 10016-8810

Distributed in Australia by Capricorn Link (Australia) Pty Ltd
2/13 Carrington Road, Castle Hill NSW 2154

A British Library Cataloguing in Publication Data block for this book may be obtained from the British Library

ISBN 0 7063 7430 4

Printed and bound in Great Britain by
Biddles Ltd, Guildford and King's Lynn

CONTENTS

INTRODUCTION

Parties are memorable experiences – for both children and adults. While I sink gratefully into a chair my children start to plan the next one the minute the last guest leaves!

One of the key ingredients to success is to tailor the party to the needs of the child. Do not expect a group of two-year-olds to sit patiently at the table for half an hour; similarly, respect the fact that a nine-year-old might prefer a special outing with a group of friends to a traditional birthday party.

Whatever happens, let the party be fun. There is no point spending long hours producing a marvellous tea only to feel upset if half of it is left. Keep your arrangements as simple as possible so that you feel relaxed and happy on the day. Fraught, tense parents will spoil the day for the birthday child.

Similarly, you must accept that accidents will happen. You will be very lucky if nothing gets spilled on the floor. If it does, mop it up quickly and do not let any guest feel guilty or upset about it. You should move valuable ornaments out of the way; if you do not and one gets broken just grin and bear it.

Finally, remember to make the party child feel special. It is easy to get so engrossed in the final preparations that you forget this is a very special day

---

HANDY HINT
If you are having a party for younger children make sure they all know where the bathroom is; you might need to ask them individually if they need to use it.

for him or her. That does not mean he should not help. Laying the table, blowing up balloons, re-arranging the furniture; all the jobs that need to be done can be part of the excitement and anticipation of this special day.

Do not be surprised, however, if there are a few tears or even a tantrum along the way. The excitement and nerves beforehand may get to the birthday child, too. Try to anticipate and prevent any situation likely to result in tears; if the worst happens, stay calm and play it down as much as possible.

The children will take their lead from the adult in charge; if you are relaxed, smiling and confident the party will be a success whatever happens.

WHAT TYPE OF PARTY?

Deciding what type of party to hold depends on the time of year, age of the child, your home situation and last, but not least, your finances. Here are a few guidelines to help you decide:

1 Fit the size and type of party to your home and budget. Use the chart on page 16 as a guide.
2 If you do not want the party at home (perhaps you are in the middle of decorating or expecting another baby), check local village halls, community centres or sports centres for hiring availability.
3 Contact local swimming pools to arrange a swimming party – and an organized tea afterwards.
4 Phone local hamburger and pizza restaurants. Some organize tea and games. *Always* take a few extras of your own – paper and crayons, a wrapped 'pass the parcel' – to fill in any gaps.
5 If it is summer, think about holding an outdoor party. If you have no garden find out about local parks, grounds of stately homes, National Trust land etc. Take a picnic tea and play Treasure Hunt, Tiny Hunt, Torn Pictures, Football Match, Tug-of-War, On and Off (see Party Games).
6 Look in your local paper and see if there is a magician or juggler who can form a focal point for the party. Do you have any talented relatives or friends who could help?
7 Hire a sports hall and hold a Match Party (see Party Themes).
8 Think about an outing or treat instead, e.g. trip to zoo, cinema, museum, theme park, theatre, roller

or ice skating, ten-pin bowling.

9 If your budget is limited, or your child has a friend with a similar birthday date, consider sharing a party. If you are hiring a hall this cuts the cost and gives you more guests to fill it up. Make sure each child has his or her own birthday cake. Make clear that guests invited by one child need not buy a present for the other.

HANDY HINT

If you are taking a group of children on an outing or trip you *must* have plenty of adult help, whether you are transporting them by car or relying on public transport. It is extremely tiring being in charge of other people's children — and too much of a responsibility to take on single-handed.

TIME OF DAY

Traditionally, parties are held in the afternoon and the meal is a party tea. This gives you plenty of time to get organized on the day, but it does mean a lot of waiting for the excited birthday child. Four and five-year olds may get so overwrought they are past their best by the time the birthday cake appears and six and seven year-olds might be too tired if it is a weekday and they are coming straight from school.

If the children are school age it is best to hold the party at the weekend. Then your partner or a friend could also be around to help and the children will be fresher.

Lunchtime parties are often very successful – and easier for the hostess. A large savoury dish – lasagne, pizza or barbecued chicken – followed by ice cream and a piece of birthday cake is easier to prepare than lots of fiddly bits for tea. Also the children are likely to be hungrier at lunchtime and your efforts in the kitchen will not be wasted. If it is a first or second birthday with lots of other mums present, this is the ideal time too – one and two-year olds are never at their best at five in the afternoon!

You also need to decide how long to make the party. As my children have got older I have found that we run out of time and can never fit in all the games we planned. However, with one, two and three-year olds I would keep the party short – between one and two hours maximum – as their span of concentration is limited and their powers of co-operation with one another are limited.

Older children can cope with two-and-a-half hours; if you are going on an outing this will take considerably longer.

RUNNING ORDER

Obviously every party is different but here is a sample running order for:

WINTER SIX-YEAR OLD PARTY

3.00pm	Guests arrive
3.05pm	Musical Statues
3.10pm	Musical Bumps
3.15pm	Team Games
	— Pass the Balloon
	— Chocolate Game
3.30pm	Simon Says
3.45pm	The Flour Game
3.55pm	Pin the Tail on the Donkey
4.05pm	Tea
4.20pm	Sing "Happy Birthday" and blow out candles
4.30pm	Make party hats, robots, animals, collages
4.50pm	Picture Consequences
5.05pm	Treasure Hunt/races/Grandmother's Footsteps in garden (if it is not raining)
5.20pm	Traffic Lights
5.25pm	Give each child whatever they made and party bag, read story
5.30pm	Home!

SUMMER FOUR-YEAR OLD PARTY

12 noon	Guests arrive
12.05pm	Find other half of picture
12.10pm	Pass the Parcel
12.15pm	Sticky Toffee
12.25pm	Row the Boat
12.30pm	Picnic lunch in garden
12.45pm	Cake and "Happy Birthday"

12.55pm Sleeping Lions
1.05pm Play in sandpit/paddling pool, trikes, bikes
1.15pm Races – running, walking, hopping, backwards, obstacle, egg and spoon
1.35pm What's the Time, Mr Wolf?
1.45pm Tiny Hunt
1.55pm Three Blind Mice – continue as children leave
2.00pm Home!

WINTER NINE-YEAR OLD PARTY

5.00pm 'Baddies' arrive
5.05pm Make eye patches/decorate ghost party bags
5.20pm Balloon Battle
5.30pm Hangman
5.40pm Captain Hook Says
5.45pm Blindfold John Brown's Body
6.00pm Supper
6.20pm Murder in the Dark
6.35pm Sardines
6.50pm Pass the Balloon
7.10pm Consequences
7.20pm Treasure Hunt (hard) – treasure can be plastic fingers, rubber noses from joke shop or chocolate money
7.30pm Home!

PARTIES FOR
THE VERY YOUNG

Your child's first birthday is a landmark. It marks your first year as a parent and his or her development from a helpless, newborn stranger to a demanding, messy member of the family.

I often feel first birthday parties should be for the mother especially – few initiation rites must be as testing as motherhood's first 12 months!

In fact, your baby could not care less if you have a party or not, although he will enjoy squeezing chocolate cake through his fingers and hair! But it is nice to celebrate and, if you have older children, they can often get quite upset if the youngest member of the family does not have a party of his own.

FIRST BIRTHDAY

- Make this a purely family get-together: if you invite aunts and grannies you will have plenty of help and can leave them entertaining the baby while you organize the cake and cups of tea.
  Or . . .
- Ask four or five other parents with babies of similar ages. You can keep it very simple and have morning coffee together with a special cake (white mouse, clown, hedgehog – see Party Cakes p. 84) and one candle.
- Try a simple lunch – chicken salad and bread for the adults and some puréed chicken and vegetables for the babies.
- Organize additional highchairs or borrow baby seats from the other mothers.
- If you invite older children you will need to organize a few games to keep them happy,

although if they are ten or eleven-year olds they
will help to keep the babies amused.
- Alternatively, get together with a few other mums
and take the babies swimming at the local pool.
Follow this with lunch at the leisure centre or a
nearby fast food restaurant (take pots of baby
food and yoghurt).

SECOND BIRTHDAY

- Two-year olds will enjoy the excitement and
atmosphere of a party, but if things get too hectic
they can easily dissolve into tears.
- Keep the party short – they will play 'alongside'
rather than 'with' each other, so have lots of
suitable toys laid out.
- Set up a 'duplo' train track and engines, a doll
corner with dolls, pushchairs, prams; (real and/or
toy ones); cooking area with pots, pans and
pretend cookers (make this from an upside down
cardboard box, draw knobs on front and four
rings on top).
- In summer, set a washing up bowl of water
outside with a few ducks and containers to hand
for filling and emptying. If you have a small
paddling pool this is ideal but supervize at all
times.
- Try to borrow a few 'sit and ride' toys, or ask
guests to bring one each. Make sure you have one
for each child if the peace is to remain unbroken!
- Sit each child on an adult's knee and play Pass the
Parcel (a sweet between each layer of wrapping
paper will help to focus their interests!).
- Play nursery rhymes and encourage children to
clap and join in.
- Provide crayons and paper for drawing.
- Blow up balloons for children to bat around. Some
may be frightened when they pop – beware!

THIRD BIRTHDAY

- At three some children will enjoy a more formal party. In fact, the guests at my son's third birthday party were the most well-mannered and polite we have ever had! Left on their own without their mums they all felt terribly 'grown-up', but they were new to the experience of going to parties and had not developed the rowdy confidence of some older children.
- Play a few very well-known games – Pass the Parcel, Musical Bumps, and What's the Time, Mr Wolf? are good ones to try. See Games for the Very Young p. 58.
- Put out building sets and puzzles for children who prefer not to join in.
- If the children are confident, let off a few party poppers, and/or throw streamers for them to unravel.
- If the weather is fine, hold races in the garden.
- If you have a sandpit and/or paddling pool let them finish the party playing in these!
- Do not try any elaborate fancy dress or theme – these children will love the novelty of a birthday party without any extra ingredients.

BEWARE: Young children are fascinated by the candle flames. You must **NEVER** let a child get near enough to touch the flame. Watch him or her for every second it is alight and make sure the extinguished candles are removed from the room immediately.

HOW MANY TO INVITE

What can you afford? Deciding on numbers can be tricky. You often feel obliged to ask certain children because they are in your child's class or because your child has been to their party. But do not overestimate how many children to invite – fit the party to the size of your home and budget.

| Child's age | Flat | Type of home | |
		Small house no garden	House with garden
3–4	5–6	5–6	8–10
5–7	8	8–10	12+
8–10	8	10	12+
10+	8	10	12+

NOTE: If you are hiring a hall you can increase these numbers but you must organize 3–4 adult helpers.

HANDY HINT
When you make up the list remember you may get several refusals, so you need to invite two or three more than your 'ideal' number. If they all accept, you will cope.

INVITATIONS

The simplest invitations to send out are those bought in pads at stationery shops. There are lots of bright designs, they are cheap and if your child is old enough he can help by writing his name and the name of the guest.

- Send out invitations 2–3 weeks before the date.
- Put your telephone number on the invitation. Children often misplace the cut-off reply slips whereas if parents can contact you direct you will get a much better idea of who is coming.
- Include the party date, start and finish times, your full address, a request to reply and any additional information, e.g. bring wellies, casual wear please (for sport party), wear something green.
- Keep a list of the children you have invited and tick off the replies as you receive them. (I once forgot to do this and got totally confused about numbers, ending up with half a dozen spare party bags, just in case!)
- One week before the party ring the parents of any guests who have not replied.
- If you are feeling very creative you may decide to make your invitations. Spaceship, wigwam, clown's face, wobbly jelly, witch, or number invitations are easy to make and look very effective

---

HANDY HINT
Do not force your child to invite
people he/she does not like. On the other
hand you cannot leave out just one child of a
group – this can be tricky to organize.

(see Party Themes for more ideas). Use glue, coloured paper, card stickers, felt pens and trace an outline from a book for your template. If you have the patience ask your child to help, although enthusiasm may wane if there is a large number!

PARTY TABLES

These should look wonderful. You can buy tablecloths, napkins, paper plates and cups linked to your theme quite cheaply; choose simple, coloured ones or make your own.

- Buy white tablecloths and cups and decorate them to fit in with your theme (see Party Themes p. 28 for ideas). Use felt tip pens on the cups – or get your children to do it – and cut out shapes like stars, moons, suns, animals, witches' faces, toys, skull and crossbones and colour them in. Then staple them to plain white paper tablecloths.
- Make place names by folding pieces of coloured paper – or transform them into crackers by drawing a cracker shape then decorating it.
- Hang streamers from the ceiling above the table or floor 'picnic'.
- Buy a helium-filled balloon for each child and let these float to the ceiling above the tea. You can take them down and present them to the children at the end of the party.

PARTY ROOM

It adds to the excitement if you can create a special party room. This could be linked to your theme – a skull and crossbones on the door for a pirate party, a cobweb hanging down for a 'spooky' or Halloween party. Or just write 'Joanna's Party' in bright, colourful letters and hang it across the door.

You can also use the front door to entice children! How about a big arrow with 'This way for Jack's party' or 'The fun starts here'.

HELPERS

- You will feel more relaxed and be able to watch some of the fun with plenty of adult help.
- Two people can run a party but if one of you is also taking photographs or making a video of the special day they will not be able to help much with the games, food and ferrying to and from the toilet.
- Invite grandparents; they often love to help. What seems like a lot of hard work and stress to you can be tremendous fun for them! But do not ask them to do too much; the noise and mess of young children can be overwhelming when you are not used to dealing with it every day.
- Organize another mum or an 'aunt' or 'uncle' if possible. Then two people can run the games while the third person finishes the last-minute preparations for the meal, welcomes late arrivals or copes with shy children.

PARTY COUNTDOWN

Everyone is different and some party hosts need to plan the day far more thoroughly than others. If you feel worried and nervous without a fairly detailed running schedule then you should compose one; but if this makes the day seem less like a fun event and more like an army exercise then do not go overboard on the strategic planning. You must have a minimum plan, even if only in your head, if you are to avoid chaos. And remember to be flexible. If the children are whooping it up playing Murder in the Dark or Blind Man's Buff you may have to drop another game so they can carry on for a bit longer. Here is a checklist you can use:

Four weeks to go
- Think about type of party, date, place, times, theme, numbers, cake.
- Book hall, leisure centre if necessary.
- Choose wet weather alternative if outside party.

Three weeks to go
- Send out invitations.
- Look for 'prizes' and 'goodies' for take-home bags. Local corner newsagents often have a marvellous selection of cheap toys, so do Woolworths. Some companies will send you a big bag of novelty toys.
- Start to plan games.
- Order a cake or find a recipe.
- Organize helpers.
- Book a video camera if you want to record the party.
- Make a shopping list for food.

HANDY HINT
When you are thinking about prizes
bear in mind the sex of the children. If your
party is mixed it is safer to choose 'unisex'
items as prizes, but if you are providing party
bags you can obviously do different ones for
boys and girls if you prefer.

Two weeks to go
- Organize costumes if theme or fancy dress, e.g. buy fangs for vampire, cut up sheet for ghost, make skeleton or dragon outfits (see Party Themes page 28).
- Make 'props' e.g. signs and decorations for party room; Pin the Tail on the Donkey board, etc.
- Buy non-perishable items for party tea e.g. ice cream cornets, paper cases, food colourings (see Party Food – Shopping on page 80).

One week to go
- Buy balloons, streamers, party paper goods. (serviettes, tablecloths).
- Decorate paper goods.
- Make as much food as possible, e.g. cheese straws, biscuits, main supper dish if you have a freezer (see Party Food – Shopping on page 80).
- Contact parents who have not replied to invitation.
- Bake cake if you have a freezer to store it in.
- Find out what is on at the cinema and/or phone local halls for availability – emergency standby.
- Buy candles, candleholders and matches for the birthday cake.
- Buy any special equipment – wool, glue, coloured stars, pillowcases etc.

One day to go
- Collect or make birthday cake.
- Prepare party bags.
- Make sure all games are organized – wrap pass-the-parcel, prepare 'memory' tray (and hide from birthday child!).
- Bake and ice cakes.
- Organize sharpened pencils and paper for written games, clues for treasure hunts.
- Prepare as much food as possible.
- Check film is in camera and/or collect hired video.
- Get emergency video tape.
- Put extra ice cubes in freezer.
- Make place names (see Party Tables page 18).
- Buy orange/blue light bulbs for special effects.

The Big Day
- Blow up balloons, put up streamers and decorations (remember to hang balloons and/or sign on front door or in garden so guests can find the house easily).
- Clear furniture, put away breakable ornaments.
- Prepare sandwiches.
- Lay the table, put out and cover all cold food.
- If you are planning to offer wine/tea to adults check provisions!
- Put musical tapes/records ready for background music.
- Change any special coloured lightbulbs.
- RELAX!

PREPARING YOUR HOME

Have everything ready before the guests arrive.

- If you have two rooms available organize the tea before the party starts and set it out.
- If you are short of chairs spread a tablecloth on the floor (put a plastic sheet underneath to protect carpet from spillages) and have a 'picnic' tea.
- If you have only one downstairs room adapt a bedroom.
- Push the bed to the side, move out all toys and easily-moveable furniture, hang a few streamers and the room will be transformed. OR . . .
- Use the garage.
- Move all furniture.
- Have bowls of sweets for prizes.

- Lay treasure hunts, wool trails, etc.
- Put up 'party room' signs.
- Check record player/cassette recorder/video is set up.

As the guests arrive make sure you are nearby and can answer the door as soon as you hear a knock. The birthday child will probably be desperate to welcome his/her guests too. If the children are older, their mother will probably stay on the doorstep but younger ones will want mums to come in and stay for a few minutes until they are settled. Start a game immediately – shy children will soon join in when they see the others having fun!

OPENING PRESENTS

Decide when you are going to allow the birthday child to open presents. Other children often enjoy watching presents being opened – particularly their own – and seeing the birthday child's pleasure.

- If he/she is very young (five and below) he will want to rip them open immediately.
- Stay with him so you can make sure he thanks each guest properly.
- Put the opened presents safely to one side once the games begin.
- Slip in very quickly if he gets a duplicate toy – "How lovely, you have got twin Postman Pats, Lion-Os (or whatever)". Warn him beforehand that all his guests have taken great time and trouble to choose presents so he must say thank you properly for all of them.
- Keep the present opening short.
- Ask one of your helpers to start a game going for those guests who are not interested in watching the ceremony!
- If the child is older, he may be persuaded to wait until the end of the party. (This means there is something else to look forward to once the last guest has gone home and it will be a calmer time for you.)
- Remember to make a list of who gave what.
- The day after the party help the birthday child to write a short thank-you note to each child. (If he is young write the notes and get him to sign them, or you can cheat and buy 'thank-you' cards but he will still have to sign his name.

PACING THE PARTY

You will need a mixture of games to suit the different personalities of the children. Some will be good at written games, others will prefer more physical activities. Some like to compete, others do not.

You will also need to alternate noisy, exciting games with quiet activities. If you are playing team games and the pitch becomes too frenetic, change the atmosphere with a quieter game.

You may want to calm the children right down before their parents arrive to collect them. It is quite good fun to end with a mad chase round the garden, but time it so they have ten minutes to get their breath back before collection time!

NAUGHTY CHILDREN

Inevitably there will be one or two 'live wires' with the potential to disrupt the party – I should know, I have one of my own!

The trick is to keep things moving so there is no opportunity for them to start playing you up. Pace the party so the children are always involved in an activity or game and you should not have too much trouble.

Play I Spy at the tea table if trouble seems to be looming; start Sleeping Lions (page 68) if a few children are taking longer to finish making hats or painting pictures.

Be on the lookout for any fighting or bullying and clamp down on it quickly. Many parents are hesitant about rebuking other people's children, but it is your responsibility to control the party. From the child's point of view a sharp reprimand from a friend's mother is often far more effective than one from their own.

SHY CHILDREN

Do not force shy children to join in. If the child is young, a cuddle on your lap can be very reassuring. He/she may prefer to watch the first few games and suddenly you will notice he has quietly joined in. Sometimes it works if you make him your helper: "Andrew, please can you hand out the sweets" or "Catherine, tell me how many people want orange juice to drink". Sitting him next to the birthday child can also be effective if he does not know many other guests.

PARTY BAGS

Unfortunately, children today seem to expect some sort of party or loot bag to take home. You may choose to disregard this tradition or substitute a simpler alternative. One year we had a huge bowl of mini-chocolate bars and the children each chose one. A friend of mine gave each child a bag of delicious home-made fudge at the end of her daughter's party. A bran tub of presents would be a novel idea – each child could pick out one to take home, or you could hold a tombola with each ticket a winner!

Finally, you could choose a take-home gift appropriate to your theme – a bag of chocolate coins for a Pirate Party (see p. 37), a plastic cowboy and Indian (see p. 45) or animal (see p. 33), or a gift of the right 'colour', e.g. pink hairslides, a green badge, blue marbles for a Colour Party (see page 35).

You can buy plastic party bags quite easily, but it is fun to make your own. Simple see-through plastic freezer bags can be transformed with a bright ribbon fastening them, or get some white paper bags (try your local shop) and decorate them individually.

PARTY THEMES

There is no end to the different ideas you can come up with for a party theme, but do remember that not all children want an elaborately planned 'original' party – many are happy with the traditional format. When I regaled my son with ideas for his fifth birthday party he pleaded, "Please Mummy, can I just have an *ordinary* party?"

Also, bear in mind that tried and tested ideas – a circus, pirates, cowboys and Indians – may sound hackneyed to us, but children adore them. That is why they have been around so long and are still so popular!

So, again, listen to what your child says. If he wants cowboys, even though it's the third cowboy party his class has attended that term, then so be it.

Of course you can always incorporate some of the theme ideas without feeling you need to follow them exactly. Clown invitations and a clown cake would work just as well. Or perhaps just ask all the children to come wearing something green for a party in the garden. If you turn to page 56 you will find some alternative ideas for Quick Themes.

BADDIES PARTY

Invitations
- Send out ghost, pirate, or evil face invitations (warty face, black teeth, stubbly hair).
- Make a spider's web, monster head or character cake (see page 92).
- Birthday child can dress up as a witch, dragon, vampire, ghost, bandit, skeleton or one of the evil TV characters. Get a picture of the character he or she chooses to copy.

Costumes

WITCH
- Make a black card pointed hat.
- Make a broomstick from piece of dowel rod, hazel twigs and string to bind it together. Make long black cloak from rectangle of black material (dyed sheet?) gathered at the neck. Make armholes so the 'witch' can join in games more easily.
- Paint black spot on face!

DRAGON
- Suggest the birthday child wears a dark green top and matching tights.
- Make a green hood and sew on two pointed ears stuffed with old tights.
- Draw scales with black felt tip pen. Draw orange flames of fire coming out of either side of his mouth.

- Make the tail from same material. Draw on scales, stuff with tights and sew.
- Make matching boots. Use large socks as pattern. Sew front and back seams, put elastic in tops.

VAMPIRE
- Make a long black cloak. Wear over a white shirt, black bow tie and black trousers.

- Buy plastic fangs from joke or toyshop and paint red blood on lips and chin. Slick back hair with gel.

GHOST
- Use old sheet cut so child will not trip. Cut out eyeholes. Fasten elastic round back of head to hold sheet in place. You can cover the sheet with black net or attach some to top of head.

BANDIT
- Large sombrero hat, old jeans, 'ethnic' top (bright cheesecloth or cotton) to hang outside jeans.
- Gun and holster.
- Make card 'spurs', cover in silver foil and stick on old wellington boots.
- Draw black stubbly chin with kohl pencil. Add an eyepatch.

SKELETON
- Get a black leotard or jersey and tights. Make white felt bones or paint on white bones.
- Draw white bones on face or you could make a black mask – use black stocking with eye and mouth holes and sew on white bones.

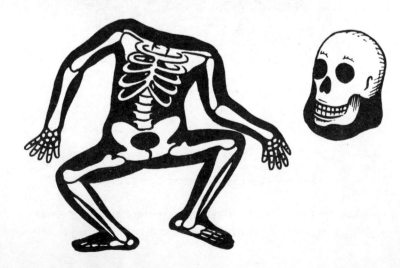

'TV' EVIL CHARACTER

- Whichever 'evil' TV character you choose they all seem to share certain characteristics. Many have breastplates, wristlets and anklets.
- Make material boots (see dragon) and some form of headdress or mask.

Use swimming trunks or underpants for the shorts and get wristlets and anklets from sports shops.

- Make breastplate from cardboard or fabric. Give your 'character' a toy version of himself to take, then everyone will see instantly who he or she is supposed to be.

Decorations

- Decorate the walls with cut-out witch, robber or ghost faces. If the children are older change the light bulbs to blue or orange or put nightlights in jam jars to cast eerie shadows (be careful of fire).
- Hang a sheet painted with a ghost shape over the party room door. Guests have to duck under it to enter.
- Make a sign saying 'Beware all who enter!'
- Hang a skeleton (made from white card 'bones' stuck onto black) outside your house instead of balloons.
- Use black paper to cover the table and use pumpkins or melons to make spooky faces.

Prizes and Going Home Presents

- Cover a wicker basket or bucket with black paper to make a witch's cauldron where you keep the prizes and/or going home gifts. Get some twigs from the garden to place beside it and have a large wooden spoon handy to 'stir' the brew.
- Buy plastic skeletons, ghost rubbers, dragon pencil sharpeners, eye patches, skeleton pens and pencils as going home presents.

Games

1 **Torchlight** (page 63)
2 **John Brown's Body** (page 74). Get an adult to dress as a ghost and pass round the items of the body for the baddies to feel
3 **Simon Says** (page 72): change to Captain Hook Says
4 **Pin the Tail on the Donkey** (change to Dragon) (page 68)
5 **Treasure Hunt** (page 69): make the 'treasure' a plastic hand or some other ghoulish object
6 **Swinging Doughnuts** (page 64) – 'handcuff' the 'baddies' hands behind their backs first
7 **Hunt the Slipper** (page 71). Instead of a slipper use a plastic sword or gun

---

BEWARE: If the children are seven or under some of these games will frighten them if played in the dark. Leave out John Brown's Body and Torchlight. Whatever the age, if any child starts to get frightened switch on the lights immediately, put on some cheery music and concentrate on 'fun' games instead.

---

8 At the end of the party get an adult to dress up as a ghost. Give the children rolls of toilet paper to catch him and tie him up.

HALLOWEEN PARTY
Adapt Baddies Party

Costumes
● Witch, vampire, ghost

Decorations
● As above

● Use nightlights, cut out faces in pumpkins or melons and put in candles

Cake
● Halloween cake (see Party Cakes on p. 84)

ANIMAL PARTY

Invitations
● Send out animal invitations. Ask the children to come dressed as animals and/or ask them all to bring a favourite animal toy.
● A variation on this theme is a 'teddy bear's picnic'. Each child brings their own teddy.
● If you have space set a place at the tea table or picnic for the toy animals or bears — or give them a little picnic of their own.

Costumes

CAT, MOUSE, BEAR
● Provide a headdress, tail and paws.
● Make the tail from a long piece of appropriately-coloured material sewn into a tube and stuffed with old tights.
● You can make 'paws' for feet by sewing sock-shaped boots (see 'baddies' costumes on page 29) and stitching on black wool for claws.
● For hands use mittens as pattern. Add pink felt circles to inside and claws.
● For headdress use grey, brown, black, white felt, cheap material or old tights with hole cut for face. Use child's hat to model size. Make chinstrap which fastens with a popper to keep headdress on. Make fur or felt ears. Cut two ear shapes, sew two edges, stuff then turn inside out and sew third edge for each ear. Attach to headdress.
● Draw whiskers onto face with face paints, eye pencils. Blacken nose, draw in eyelashes.

- For rest of body get child to wear tights and leotard, t-shirt or jersey in same colour.

ZEBRA
- Wear stripey leggings and jersey (you could add white felt strips to black jersey).
- Make tail from strands of black wool doubled and bound together at the top. Stitch or pin to tights.
- Stick black wool mane to top and back of headdress.

HORSE
- Make mane and tail as above.
- Add fetlock hair by making anklets from elasticated material.
- Stick on short pieces of wool.

HANDY HINT
The younger the children, the simpler the costume should be. Just a headdress and painted whiskers can look very effective.

Decorations
Cardboard animal shapes stuck on walls and above door of party room — fishes, lions, cats!

- Hang spiders, butterflies and birds from ceiling.
- Put birthday child's toy animals around edges of the room.

Games

1 **What's the Time, Mr Wolf?** (page 60)
   Change the name to the right animal, e.g. 'What's the time Mr Zebra?
2 **Noisy Stories** (page 61)
   Give each child the noise most appropriate to their costume
3 **Poor Pussy** (page 67)
4 **Team Races** (page 65)
   Put children into 'animal' teams for all team games, e.g. dogs and cats, cats and mice, foxes and rabbits
5 **Cat and Mouse** (page 69)
   (Change to whatever the animals are, e.g. bear growls, horse neighs, rabbit goes 'map map')
6 **Musical Bumps/Statues** (page 62)
   When you sit down/stand still you must make your own animal noise

Cake

Make animal cake – sausage dog, rabbit, ladybird, butterfly (see Party Cakes page 84).

Music

Use animal music as background, e.g. 'Old Macdonald had a Farm', 'How Much is that Doggy in the Window?', 'There Once Was an Ugly Duckling', 'Teddy Bear's Picnic', 'Me and my Teddy Bear', 'Puff the Magic Dragon', 'The Unicorn Song'.

COLOUR PARTY

Choose the birthday child's favourite colour as your 'theme' (persuade him/her not to choose black or dark brown if possible!).

Invitations

Send out invitations in the chosen colour, ask guests

to wear something in that colour – it need only be socks or a hairslide.

Decorations
Decorate party room with streamers and balloons in the theme colour.

Activity
● Provide cardboard 'hats' or crowns – not stuck together.
● Issue paper, stars in appropriate colour (perhaps add some gold and silver for a bit of variety), felt tip pens in 'theme colour'.
● Get the children to decorate the hats then glue or staple them to fit each child's head.

Games
1 **Pass the Parcel** (page 58)
● Wrapped in theme colour with theme-coloured prize.
2 **Twenty Items** (page 75)
● Write down (or draw) 20 items of the appropriate colour.
3 **Treasure Hunt** (page 69)
● Scatter pieces of paper of the appropriate colour. Once these are all collected and pieced together turn over for the clue to find the hidden treasure.
● Have 'forfeit' trail-paper of a different colour torn and scattered. Once these are collected and pieced together the message on the back should read something like 'You followed the wrong colour trail so your prize will be . . . To write blue (or whatever the theme colour is) 15 times N-E-A-T-L-Y!
4 **Wool Gathering** (page 72)
● Wool of the appropriate colour has a prize; all other colours have booby prizes, e.g. carrots!

Food

TEA

- Serve theme-coloured jelly (if pink make a milk jelly), iced biscuits, ice cream and fruit.

LUNCH

- Prepare appropriate-coloured dips, e.g. tomato, ham, green peppers with vegetables.
- Make theme-coloured drinks and ice cubes by adding a few drops of food colouring to lemonade and ice cubes.

CAKE

- Colour cake (see Party Cakes page 92).

HANDY HINT

If it's summer time, pre-arrange with your local ice cream van to drive up and serve pink (or vanilla or chocolate) cornets to the children from the van.

PIRATE PARTY

A great favourite! Pirate parties are still extremely popular today and they are fun to hold too. Costumes are simple to make yet very effective and traditional 'treasure hunt' games can be prepared with confidence, knowing children will enjoy every minute! This theme is perfect for an outdoor party, but the games can be adapted for indoor use too.

Invitations

- Send pirate faces, 'black spots' (if children have not read *Treasure Island* you will need to add a line explaining 'You are a marked man/woman').
- Make an eye patch for each child and write the party details on the back.

Costume
- Make eye patch from black paper or material fastened to black ribbon/elastic.
- Buy or make card admiral hat or tie a scarf over hair and fasten at nape of neck.
- Tie striped scarf round neck.
- Wear clip-on gold earring.
- Blacken a tooth with kohl eye pencil!
- Wear a striped T-shirt, cut-off denim shorts or black leggings and canvas shoes.
- Bring a toy parrot along too!

Decorations
- Hang a skull and crossbones shape outside the house and/or over the party room door. Decorate plain white tablecloth with skull and crossbones.

Games
1 **Obstacle race** (page 63)
  Get the children to put on a pirate's hat, tuck a (toy!) parrot under their arm, balance along a plank supported on old tyres, take off shoes and jump into a low tub of water, fill bucket with sand, etc. This game is best played outside!
2 **Tug of War** (page 66)
3 **Ship Ahoy** (page 73)
4 **Treasure Hunt** (page 69)
  Use gold chocolate coins for treasure.

5 **Sand and Water** (page 64)
6 **Pin the Tail on the Donkey** (page 68)
   Adapt to Pin the Parrot on the Pirate's Shoulder
7 **Shipwreck** (page 72)
8 **On and Off** (page 73)
   Change to On Board. Lay a blanket on the floor
   for the pirate ship. Commands are 'On Board'
   and 'Into the Sea!'

Finale
If it is a very hot day and you are feeling charitable,
end the party as a marauding pirate being chased by
the 'other' pirates plus hosepipe. The aim is to grab
the pipe and turn it on them.
NOTE: Lots of these games involve rushing
around. Intersperse with quieter ones too or the
guests will not survive the pace!

Tea
• Decorate plain white tablecloths with skull and
  crossbones. Make skull-faced sandwiches with
  carrot crossbones crossed beneath – or do same
  with jacket potatoes and sausages.
• Pirate cake or treasure chest cake (see Party Cakes
  pages 91 and 93).

CELEBRITY PARTY

Invitations
- Use thick card and curly writing like an invitation to a ball.
- Ask children to come as their favourite celebrity to the Anniversary Ball.
- As children arrive take a polaroid photograph of them, like film stars arriving at a premiere. Save these, and give them to them with party bags.

Costumes
- Obviously these depend on the child's chosen celebrity, but striking make-up for pop stars, and extra smart clothes for TV stars are good guidelines. Top hats, handbags, dark glasses, and cardboard hand-held microphones could be useful props.

Decorations
- Posters of current pop stars on the wall. Signed pictures of TV stars (most TV stations will send you some) will add a touch of glamour, and will make excellent prizes, too.

Games
1 **Who Am I?**
   As each child has come as celebrity, why not ask them to act out the person so that everyone can guess who they are.
2 **Grandmother's Footsteps** (page 64)
   Change the name to Pop Star's Footsteps – all the other celebrities have to compete to become the top star by tapping him or her on the shoulder.
3 **Finding Out** (page 65)
   Instead of using a newspaper, buy a copy of a pop paper or *Radio* or *TV Times* and ask questions about that.

Music
- Use disco or film music as a background. After all, this is a celebrity party and they all go to nightclubs or appear in films.
- Have some fanfare music to greet each guest's arrival!

COME TO THE CIRCUS

Invitations
- Use a circus-type illustration, perhaps of a ringmaster
- Make invitations in the form of tickets to the circus.
- Ask the children to come dressed as anything they like from one of the animals, a clown, a trapeze artist, even the ringmaster.

Costumes

Ringmaster
Top hat, tails, and a stick with a bit of string tied to one end. Children can take it in turns to wear the hat and hold the whip and whoever is ringmaster can be in charge of the next game.

Trapeze artist
A leotard with added glitter – or festooned with any kind of decoration that sparkles.

Clown
At the very least, wear a red plastic nose. Clown faces should be white with an oversize mouth and nose and big eyes. Wear big, baggy trousers and enormous shoes, perhaps with a big bow on them. A huge floppy bow tie will complete the outfit.

Decorations
- If the party is outside, put out a circle of sawdust to make a ring for the games.

- Inside, lots of streamers will create the effect of the big tent.
- Put round big cartons of popcorn for the children to help themselves during the party.

Games

1 **Chocolate Game** (page 65)
Change the outfit to a baggy clown's suit.
2 **Team Races** (pages 65–68)
Change the name to a circus animal, juggler or clown.
3 **Musical Hats** (page 63)
Have a ringmaster's top hat to pass around to the music.
4 **Traffic Lights** (page 68)
Change to Circus Tent and divide the children into teams of Lions, Clowns and Ringmasters. Each has to find their team by shouting their name.
5 **Swinging Doughnuts** (page 64)

Music

- Any fairground-type music will make the perfect background.

Tips

- As a surprise, you could fill up some buckets with small pieces of torn-up paper and then come rushing out and .throw them around. This is safe and very exciting for children – and less messy than water.
- Announce all stages of the party – from games to tea time – in the pompous manner of a ringmaster "Ladies and gentlemen, I present for your delight and amusement, a special birthday cake."

Cake

- Clown cake (see Party Cakes page 89)

COLLAGE PARTY

Invitations

1 Stick coloured paper, egg box cups, corks, material onto cards to make a picture (party hat, cake).
2 Cut up small pieces of material (an old sheet), cover card, stick design on one side, use indelible marker to write party details on reverse.

As They Arrive

- Provide piles of coloured paper, tissue paper, wool, string, ribbon, rice, beans, pasta, pipe cleaners, old cards, paint, felt tip pens, crayons.
- Get each child to make their own collage picture.
- All work together to produce a giant collage (pin a huge sheet of thick paper to the wall – not a newly decorated one!)
- This can be a specific character or scene linked to the party theme, e.g. a nativity scene (Christmas party), or rabbit (animal party).
- Draw an outline in black felt tip pen; give each child an area to 'fill in' or make it 'abstract' so the children can make their own pattern or figure.

Games

1 **Chocolate Game** (page 65).
   Use pieces of white/milk/plain chocolate.
2 **Sausages** (page 67).
   Change to 'Patchwork'.
3 **Pin the Tail on the Donkey** (page 68).
   Make collage donkey.
4 **Treasure Hunt** (page 69).
   Make collage clues.
5 **On and Off** (page 73).
   Use patchwork quilt.

Cake

Paintbox (page 93).

SPACE PARTY

Invitations

Send rocket-shaped invitations.
- Draw and colour.
- Use card covered with silver foil. Write details on reverse.

Decorations

- Hang rocket on front door/door of party room.
- Hang moon and star shapes cut from coloured card on thread from ceiling.

Tea

- Cover table with silver foil.
- Use silver foil containers.
- Spread blue (space-coloured) streamers on table for colour variety.

Astronaut Costume

- Use silver material to make top and trousers OR
- Cover card breastplate shape in silver foil.
- Paint old wellington boots/trainers with silver paint. Add stars.
- Make helmet from silver stocking – cut out face shape. Pull over head.
- Wear gloves.

Prizes

Anything silver! Try silver/gold pencils, crayon sets, figures, cars, hairslides.

Games

1 **Chocolate Game** (page 65).
   Put on silver helmet (use plastic cooking bowl covered in foil) and gloves.
2 **Ship Ahoy** (page 73).
   Change to 'The Aliens are Coming'.

3 **Simon Says** (page 72).
Change to 'Simon Spaceman Says'.
4 **Memory Game** (page 76).
Use items an astronaut would need in his rocket,
e.g. toothbrush, packet soup, bar of soap, flask,
etc.
5 **Balloon Battle** (page 67).
Rename 'Aliens v Astronauts'.
6 **Treasure Hunt** (page 69).
Make 'alien clues', i.e. instead of writing or
drawing 'tree' say 'a tall brown pole growing out
of the earth with green on top'.

Tea

1 Make green ice cubes for drinks, serve rocket ice
lollies in summer.
2 Serve ice cream shaped as a moon monster.

Cake

Space rocket (see Party Cakes page 86).

COWBOYS AND INDIANS PARTY

Invitations

● Coloured feather with initial tied to it.
● Sheriff's badge.
● Piece of 'parchment' (wet paper then dry on
radiator – make 'bullet hole' with hole punch).

Costumes

COWBOY

● Buy cowboy hat (or make or adapt a felt hat using
cord tassle round brim and putting gold star in the
middle).
● Tie spotted scarf round neck.
● Wear checked shirt, jeans and waistcoat.
● Buy toy holster and gun.

INDIAN
- Buy headdress from toyshop (squaws can use soft hairband worn like headband with a single feather stitched to the back).
- Paint face with bright face pencils/kohl pencils.
- You can buy Indian 'suede-type' jerkins and trousers or adapt an old top. It should be plain. Add a suede or leather belt at the waist.
- Boys can wear jeans or black leggings.
- Add a necklace and wristlet of ethnic beads.

Decorations
Stick feathers in the hedge or around front door frame and party room door.

Music
'She'll be Coming Round the Mountain' and any music from Western films, e.g. 'Whip Crack Away', 'Two Wheels on My Wagon' etc.

Games
1 **On and Off** (page 73).
   All the children are cowboys or 'scout Indians'. The blanket is the stage coach. If you shout 'On the stage coach' the children must stay off the blanket and vice versa.
2 **Ship Ahoy** (page 73).
   Change to Apaches are Coming!
3 **Treasure Hunt** (page 69).
   Use feathers – different colours for different teams with clues attached – to lead to the treasure – a collection of miniature cowboy and Indian figures (one for each child).
4 **Simon Says** (page 72).
   Change to 'Cowboy Joe Says'. Ask guests to make an Indian noise, lassoo a steer, drink an ice-cold beer (mime the actions as you speak).

5 **Guess the Shout/Laugh/Snort** (page 78).
Change to Indian Warcry. Divide players into two
teams. One team is blindfolded. One by one they
listen to the other team making warcry noises.
6 **Blindfold Drawing** (page 77).
Draw a picture of a cowboy. Add an Indian, a
teepee, a horse, a sheriff's badge on the cowboy, a
peace pipe. Give the prize to the best drawing.

Food
Serve hamburgers, hot dogs or barbecued chicken.

Drinks
● Old-fashioned lemonade, ginger beer, milk shake
or cola. Finish with banana ice cream with
butterscotch sauce.

Cake
● Wigwam (page 88).
● Character Indian cake (page 92)
● Character-cowboy (page 92).
● Borrow trestle tables and chairs and cover tables
with checked tablecloths. Put little vases of flowers
on top for 'saloon' effect.

MATCH PARTY
For older children a football/cricket/rounders match
party can be great fun – and an ideal way to burn
off all their excess energy too!

● Use a local park or recreation ground or hire a
football or cricket pitch (or a five-a-side complex
in a sports centre).
● Check if any kitchen facilities are available. If not
you will need to pack a complete picnic tea.
● Remember they will be very thirsty after the match
– take lots to drink.

Invitations
● A cricket bat, football or baseball bat.
● Ask children to come in appropriate gear and bring any equipment (e.g. cricket bats).

Games
The 'match' will take up most of the time. However, if you are playing football with eight-year olds cut down the time to two 20-minute halves. You will probably have smaller teams too.

Refreshments
Provide wedges of orange and plenty of cold drinks for half-time.
After the match and tea you can play a few quieter games:

1 **I Went to Peru** (page 75).
2 **Charades** (page 73).
3 **Open-air Treasure Hunt** (page 69) leading to a football, cricket pads or whatever is appropriate.

Cake
Soccer ball (page 88).

NOTE:
● Have emergency plans if there is a downpour.
● Switch to a leisure centre or community hall.
● Eat food indoors.
● Go to the cinema.
● Hire a video.
● Plan an indoor games tournament.

1 Set up cards, board games, computer games, Subbuteo, Scalextrix, quizzes.
2 Include skipping, press-ups and 'touch your toes' sessions.
3 Pair off players, put them in teams or let them

compete individually.

4 Prepare games sheets to mark off scores for each team or player.

5 Put five or ten-minute time limits on board games (snakes and ladders, draughts, ludo).

6 Have a 'Victor Ludorum' prize for overall winner.

PYJAMA PARTY

Invitations

Send out pillowcase-style invitations.

- Sew up mini-pillowcases, write the details on the outside in indelible marker and stuff with foam pieces and old tights.
- Ask guests to wear pyjamas!
- Make Wee Willie Winkie nightcaps out of left over material.

Timing

Hold the party later than usual – say 6–8pm. The guests will feel very grown up!

As They Arrive

- Give them each a pillowcase to decorate. Either use up old ones, make up out of old sheet or buy cheap white ones.
- Provide pretty ribbons, stripey tape, buttons, beads, thread, markers (check first that they write well on the material) and felt pieces.

Decorations

Make a 'Bedroom' sign to hang over party room door. You could hang a few pillowcases on a washing line in the corner – these will be used in a game.

Make the table look like a bed! Use low table, cover with sheets and seat guests on pillows – if there is room put a pillow at one end of the table.

Food
See Suppers (page 80) for ideas.

Cake
Record cake (page 92) or Crackerjack (page 86).

Games
1 Hunt the Slipper (page 71).
2 Simon Says (page 72).
3 'Squeak Piggy Squeak' (page 69).
4 Dressing up Game (page 77).
5 Treasure Hunt (page 69).
6 Pillowcase Game (page 76).
  Stuff with bedtime items, e.g. soap, flannel, toothbrush.

Party Bags
Give small bars of soap, flannels, toothpaste.

SLEEPOVER PARTY
- This is similar to above but the guests stay the night!
- Invite fewer guests (6–8) and ask them all to bring sleeping bags.
- Hire a video for them to watch so they can 'wind down', while lying in their sleeping bags.
- Be prepared for a wakeful night – there may be lots of gigglings and whisperings.

HANDY HINT
If it is summer the children could 'camp' in the garden. You will need an adequate sized tent. Leave an outside kitchen light on – expect frequent trips back and forth to the loo.

DISCO PARTY

Invitations
- Send out jazzy invitations using glitter.
- Make black record-shaped card invitations writing details on the back.

Costumes
Sophisticated disco gear.

GIRLS
- Make a full skirt from net and satin-type material.
- Transform an ordinary outfit with sparkling tights, belt and headband.
- Glittery eyeshadow, glitter on hair, 'moondust' on cheeks!

BOYS
- Make or buy satin-type braces in bright colours.
- Wear 'liquorice tie' with white shirt.
- Gel hair.

The children will feel very grown-up!

Games
See Games for Older Children (page 73).

1 **Dancing**
- Let them enjoy dancing to the music for a while. You do not need to organize every second!
- Have dancing competitions – best dancer, best pair, longest non-stop dancing time (put a limit of 10/15 minutes on this if you do not want to exhaust your guests!).
- Best DJ. Give each guest a turn at announcing and choosing records.
2 **Musical Statues/Bumps/Islands/Chairs** (page 62). Musical games are much more grown-up to disco music. See the fun!

3 Musical Quiz Game
- Play a snatch of a record and get the children to write down the group/singer.
- Ask them to complete a verse from a current 'pop' theme.
- Get them to write out their favourite carol in full.
- Sing the rest of the line from a record.

Decorations
- Shiny streamers
- Change the lightbulbs.
- Make a 'disco deck' for the record player. Cover a table with black paper, cut out sign – 'Debbie's Dancing Disco' in silver – and stick to front.
- Put up some posters of current pop favourites.

Meal
- Set up a buffet table with sandwiches (page 00). Make plain paper plates look like record discs. Cover table with silver foil.
- Have bowls of bright orange and green (carrot and celery) raw vegetable sticks.

Drinks
Make coloured 'cocktail drinks'. Frost tops of glasses – dip in egg white then sugar – to serve lime, cherry, strawberry cocktails (mix with lemonade).

NOTE: To adapt to 'Bonfire Party'. Make firework invitations. Children will need warm clothes, not disco gear, but after fireworks and bonfire hold a disco to warm everyone up.

DINNER PARTY
A very sophisticated party for older children. If the birthday child has been involved in the preparations when you invite friends to dinner, he or she will be thrilled to have their very own evening dinner!

Invitations

BOYS
● Send out bow-tie shaped invitations.

GIRLS
● High heeled shoe-shaped invitations.

Costumes

Look through your dressing-up box.

GIRLS
Adapt a long dress; buy some glittering tights and a material flower to pin to the front.

BOYS
Borrow dad's bow-tie – or buy a cheap coloured one. Use a white (school?) shirt, slick back hair and beg, borrow or adapt a black jacket.

Decorations

Candles in the dining room. Put on an elegant tablecloth and vases of flowers.

As They Arrive

Offer them a 'drink' (see Disco Party 'cocktails') and nuts and nibbles, play background music.

Games

See Games for Older Children (page 73).

1 **Charades** (page 73)
2 **Fizzbuzz** (page 75)
3 **Murder in the Dark** (page 74)
   Great fun – watch no-one gets really scared!
4 **Sardines** (page 72)
5 **Adverbs** (page 74)

Meal

Cut down on the cooking by ordering a pizza or

Chinese takeaway and get the guests to choose the menu. You need to provide a starter – prawn cocktail or melon, and desserts – fruit salad, cheesecake, chocolate mousse.

CHRISTMAS PARTY

My daughter has a birthday in December and despite the extra work of a party in the Christmas month, it seems a very special time of year to celebrate. However, you do not need a birthday in the family to hold a Christmas Party!

Invitations
● Snowman.
● Christmas tree.
● Christmas stockings.
● Father Christmas.
Use glitter, cotton wool, for 'Christmassy' effects.

Decorations
● Put up your Christmas decorations and tree. Put going home presents under the tree and hang chocolate figures on branches for children to take.
● If it is early in December dig out your Christmas tree lights and stick them round the windows.
● Put crackers on the table.

Games
1 **Chocolate Game** (page 65)
   Each child has to 'pull a cracker' as well as putting on hat and gloves before cutting up the chocolate.
2 **Pillowcase Game** (page 76)
   Hide little 'stocking filler' presents in the pillowcase – once they have all been guessed each child can put a hand in and take one.
3 **Torn Pictures** (page 70)
   Use Christmas cards. If the children are old

enough ask each pair to make up a Christmas rhyme for inside the card.

4 **Pin the Tail on the Donkey** (page 68)
Change to 'Pin the Star on the Christmas Tree'.

5 **Ship Ahoy** (page 73)
Change to 'Father Christmas is Coming!'
When you have a winner, dim the lights, ring a bell and get an adult dressed as Father Christmas to come in and give him/her the prize. Make sure there are gifts for all the losers too!

6 **Sausages** (page 67)
Change to 'Merry Christmas'.

7 **Traffic Lights** (page 68)

As They Arrive
Make Christmas cards. Provide different-coloured glitters, gold, silver and red stars, pens, Christmas-tree template if the children are young.

Costumes
Father Christmas and snowman costumes are fun but rather cumbersome items for games. The children will probably already have been shepherds and angels in school nativity plays. Give each child a piece of tinsel to use as a headband, belt or necklace to add to the festive atmosphere.

Cake
● Christmas tree (page 93) my daughter's all-time favourite. Get the birthday child to make a gold star for the top.
● Crackerjack (page 86).

QUICK PARTY THEMES

As I pointed out in the introduction to Party Themes, you may not want to run the whole idea of a theme through your party. If you just want an idea to get the party going – or to add some atmosphere – here are some suggestions to start you off.

BIG SHOES
Children love wearing adult's shoes, and it is great fun to invite them (on a large, shoe-shaped card of course) to come along with a huge pair of shoes. They can take them off after a while, or swap with other children. You can base several of the team games on pairs of shoes and you could keep all the prize sweets in a large boot to retain the theme.

SWAPSIES
Children love swapping things, and they are always collecting something. A swapsies party can involve all of them bringing things to swap (make sure their parents approve of what they bring to barter with).

TRAFFIC LIGHTS
These make an excellent theme for invitations, dressing up, multi-coloured food, and games (see Party Games, page 58. Keep everything red, orange or green, from the food (lots of ketchup, pineapple and apples – not all in the same dish!), to the wrapping paper for Pass the Parcel.

LONG AS A PIECE OF STRING
How long is a piece of string? Find the answer at your own party! Invitations, accompanied of course by a length of string, should tell each child to come

wearing a long piece of string. The first game could be to watch them all unravel and find out who had the longest piece! The string theme could extend to knot-tying contests, or a game in which various partners are tied up with string and have to escape, or the Frozen Key game (page 67).

WRONG TIME OF YEAR

Children seem to love wacky, silly ideas, and what could be sillier than having the wrong time of year as your theme? The food can be unseasonal (turkey is available all year, and snowball shapes are easy to make from marshmallows or egg whites as meringues). The guests' clothes can be unseasonal – from swimsuits to woolly scarves.

MULTILAYERS

A fine theme for dressing up and food, and your invitations can be multilayer too – just use thin paper and write a few words on each page, and your invitation will be several sheets deep. Multilayer foods such as trifle, jellies full of different colours, even lasagne, make it an easy theme.

WHEELS

Send out circle-shaped invitations to the party, telling everyone to arrive on wheels. They can turn up on roller skates, skateboards, and bicycles, and as long as you have room for them to play, with perhaps an expedition to the park, the party will roll along very enjoyably. Try to keep all the food circular – biscuits, burgers, cakes, and so on.

COLOURS OF THE RAINBOW

The colours of the rainbow make lovely decorations for invitations, presents and food. You can ask guests to come as one or all of the colours.

PARTY GAMES

The key to success is choosing a mixture of games so every child has a chance to win. If tempers get short and children become anxious instead of enjoying the fun switch the game immediately.

You must supervize closely. Make sure no-one is hurt in the hustle and bustle of the rougher games and mix up the teams and pairs in the quieter games so no-one is left out.

FOR THE VERY YOUNG

At a two-year old's party you should aim to play two or three of these at the most; by the time the children are three and four they will enjoy them all!

Ring-a-ring of Roses
Join hands and walk round in a circle singing:
>   'Ring-a-ring of roses,
>   A pocket full of posies,
>   A-tishoo, A-tishoo,
>   We all fall down'

Then all the children sit on the floor, singing;
>   'The cows are in the meadow
>   Eating buttercups,
>   A-tishoo, A-tishoo,
>   We all jump up'

All stand up and repeat.

Pass the Parcel
Wrap up a prize (gear to the age of the children) in layers of wrapping paper. Make sure there is one layer for each guest. Put a sweet in between each layer (for older children you could make this a forfeit, e.g. 'stand on one leg', 'hum a tune', etc.).

HELPING HAND
If you do not have lots of wrapping paper use
pretty paper for the outside layer and paper
bags for the rest. The children really won't
notice the difference in their rush to unwrap
a layer!

Pass the parcel round to music. Each time the
music stops the person holding the parcel has to
unwrap a layer and eat the sweet (or carry out the
forfeit).

With younger children make sure each child has a
go then turn your back to stop the music for the last
time so the winner is a real surprise!

Knife, Fork, Spoon

A variation on 'Simon Says' in which the caller
simply says 'knife' (meaning stand upright with arms
up), 'fork' (spread the arms) or spoon (curve the
arms into a circle). Anyone who is slow to react or
makes the wrong move is eliminated until one
winner remains.

Blowing Bubbles

Get a pot of bubble-blowing liquid. Blow lots of
bubbles in the air for the children to catch.

NOTE: Try it out first — some are better than
others at producing bubbles.

Sticky Toffee

A form of tag in which anyone touched by the
person who is 'it' must stand still with legs and arms
apart. If someone scurries through their legs, they
are free to play again, if not, you will end up with a
field full of immobilized children!

Row the Boat

Get children into pairs, sitting opposite each other with legs straight out. Get them to hold hands and row gently back and forth while you all sing:
'Row, row, row the boat
Gently down the stream
Merrily, merrily, merrily, merrily
Life is but a dream'

Three Blind Mice

One player is the farmer's wife. The others form a circle round the wife and repeat Three Blind Mice. At the end of the rhyme the children run away and the farmer's wife tries to catch them. The first one caught is the farmer's wife next time. Players are safe when they touch the wall.

What's the Time, Mr Wolf?

NOTE: A favourite with older children too. One child is the wolf. He stands at the end of the room/garden facing away from the guests while the other children creep up on him chanting 'What's the time, Mr Wolf?' when he turns round they must freeze. He shouts 'Ten o'clock', 'Half-past three', but when he shouts 'Dinner Time' all the children run. He has to catch one who is the next wolf.

Fish Racing

Cut a number of kipper shapes out of a sheet of newspaper, and issue one rolled up newspaper for each fish. The game is to beat the floor behind your fish, moving it along to an agreed finishing post. Children may need some help with this.

Hokey Cokey

Great fun – watch that the children do not bash each other too hard as they move in to the centre of

the circle for the chorus!
   Stand in a circle. Sing and act out the following:
   'Put your left hand in
Your left hand out
In, out, in, out
Shake it all about
Do the Hokey Cokey (*wiggle*)
And you turn around
That's what it's all about!'
Join hands for the chorus –
   'Oh the Hokey Cokey
   Oh the Hokey Cokey
   Knees bend, arms stretch
   Ra-ra-ra'
As you sing the chorus move in and out to the centre
of the circle.
Then work your way through the body; right hand,
left foot, right foot, left leg, right leg, whole self
(jump in and out of circle).

Here We Go Round the Mulberry Bush
Join hands, walk in a circle and sing:
   'Here we go round the mulberry bush
   The mulberry bush, the mulberry bush
   Here we go round the mulberry bush
   On a cold and frosty morning'
Then make up new verses and act them out, e.g.
This is the way we ... 'Eat our toast', 'Put on our
coat', 'Walk to school', etc. Keep going while the
children are enjoying it!

Noisy Stories
Sit the children on the floor and tell a story with lots
of noises. Choose an animal or car theme – with
ducks quacking, cars tooting, fire engines dinging,
etc., and give each child a noise. At the appropriate
part of the story, Emma says 'Quack', Matthew says

'Toot toot' etc. When you say 'Good morning' (or choose another catch phrase) all the children make their noises together!

NOTE: Plan the story carefully so each child gets at least two chances to make their own noise.

MUSICAL GAMES

Musical Bumps
Get the children to jump up and down while music plays. When the music stops everyone has to sit down on the floor. The last one down is out. Continue until you have a winner.

As the children get older you can make the game more complicated, e.g. sit down and 'squawk like a chicken' or 'spell your name' etc.

Musical Statues
As above, but the children must freeze when the music stops. Anyone who moves is out.

You can make this more interesting by trying to get the children to move, e.g. 'Joanna, there is a spider on your nose' etc.

Musical Chairs
Line up two rows of chairs back to back. Have one less chair than the number of players. Get the children to circle the chairs and when the music stops they have to sit down. Anyone without a chair is out. Reduce number of chairs until you have one chair and two players left. Whoever gets to it first is the winner.

Musical Islands
Scatter pieces of paper on the floor round the room. When the music stops each player has to jump onto an island. Anyone not on an island is out. Reduce

the islands so there is always one less than the number of players.

Musical Numbers
When the music stops shout a number: 'Twos' 'Fives', etc and the children have to get into groups of that number. Those not in a group are out.

Musical Hats/Shoes
Sit children in a circle. Pass round hats or big shoes – the funnier the assortment, the better! Have one fewer item than players. When the music stops anyone without a hat or shoe on is out. Continue until you have a winner.

Torchlight
Turn down the lights and put on music. The torch is passed from player to player. Whoever is holding the torch when the music stops is out.

RACES
There is no end to the variety of races you can enjoy.
Try walking, hopping, jumping, backwards races – anyone who cheats is out!

Obstacle race
This is great fun. Borrow hoops, tunnels, tyres, lay out old clothes and use your imagination to make a fun obstacle course. The older the children, the harder it can be.

Egg and Spoon race (a)
Give each child a spoon with a hardboiled egg (some people substitute small potatoes or even chocolate eggs). The object is to run from one end of the room/garden to the other without dropping the egg. The first one there wins.

Egg and Spoon race (b)
If you do not have much space, line up two teams.
Give everyone a spoon to hold in their mouths. The
first player has the egg in his spoon and must pass it
to the next player's spoon without touching it. The
first team to pass it down the line is the winner.

Sand and Water
Divide children into two teams. Place two large
buckets/containers at one end of the garden and give
each team a small bucket. In between, place the
sandpit. The aim is to fill the large containers as
quickly as possible with sand — repeat using water
from the paddling pool.

Tortoise race
In this race the slowest competitor wins! However,
no-one must stop or weave; they must move
forward in a straight line.

One minute to go
The aim is to get from one end of the room/garden
to the other in exactly one minute. An adult must
time the race and note which competitor is closest to
the minute time allowed.

Grandmother's Footsteps
One person is grandmother and turns his back to the
rest. They have to slowly creep up on him. Every
time he turns they must stand still. If he sees anyone
moving they go back to the beginning. The player
who taps grandmother on the shoulder is the winner
and becomes the next grandmother.

Swinging Doughnuts
Thread doughnuts on pieces of string. Fasten string
to a piece of wood. Suspend from ceiling or place

across the top of two doors, or balance across chairs. Players have to eat doughnuts with hands tied behind them. First to finish wins!

TEAM RACES

Chocolate Game

Line up two teams. At the other end of the room on a table place two bars of chocolate on plates. Lay a knife and fork by each plate. On the floor in front of the table put a hat and an oversize pair of gloves.

When you say 'Go' the first player in each team has to run to the table, put on the hat and gloves, pick up the knife and fork and eat a piece of chocolate. When he has got a piece he takes off the hat and gloves, runs to the back of his team and the next player goes.

The first team to all get a piece of chocolate are the winners.

Finding Out

An excellent quiet game to calm everybody down a bit. Break the party up into teams and give every team one copy of the same day's newspaper. Then you simply ask questions prepared from the paper: how much does it cost, where is it printed, and questions based on stories in the paper. Each team has one leader who writes down the answer on a piece of paper and brings it to the quizmaster.

Pass the Ball/Balloon

The two teams stand in a row. On the word 'Go' the front player passes the ball/balloon/orange over his head to the player behind. When the last player catches it he runs to the front of the line and does the same.

This continues until the original leader is back at the front. The first team to finish wins the game.

NOTE: Vary this by getting the children to pass the balloon alternatively overhead and between legs. When the team leader returns to the front all the team stand astride while he bats the balloon through their legs to be caught by the back player.

Orange Chins

Divide into two teams. Give each leader an orange tucked under his chin. On the word 'Go' he must pass it to the next team member and so on. When it gets to the back the player must walk to the front with the orange under his chin. Continue until the original leader is back at the front.

The Nursery Rhyme Game

Divide the party into teams, and ask the members to recite one nursery rhyme after another – but the team cannot repeat a rhyme it has already recited. Do allow them to confer – there will always be one child who finds someone else has already recited the only rhyme they know!

Feed the Baby

Divide the children into pairs of boys and girls. The 'mummies' sit at one end of the room, each holding a bib and a baby's bottle half-full of milk or lemonade. The 'babies' stand at the other end of the room. When you say 'Go' they have to run to the 'mummies' who put on the bibs and feed the babies. The first to finish, remove bib and run back to other end of room wins.

Tug of War

Divide children into two teams and give each team one end of a long rope. Put a white handkerchief on the ground and check that the middle of the rope is over it. When you say 'Go' both teams pull and the team which pulls the other one over the white line wins.

Balloon Battle
Each guest has a balloon tied to his ankle and holds a rolled-up newspaper. Divide into teams, then guests try to burst the other team's balloons while protecting their own using the newspaper. No hand-touching is allowed.

Frozen Key
Put a key in the freezer a day before the party. For the game, take it out and tie a long piece of string to it. Then you line up the guests (into two teams if you like – you will need two keys) and they have to pass the key underneath their clothes down their bodies and on to the next person!

Sausages
One guest is chosen to answer everyone else's questions. Whatever the question, he or she has to reply 'Sausages!' without smiling or laughing. The other guests think up outrageous questions to make him/her laugh. When he laughs he is out and someone else has a turn.

Straight Faces
Divide into two teams. One team must tell funny jokes and make silly noises to make the other team laugh. As soon as anyone smiles or laughs they are out. Continue until all the team have laughed; the teams change places.

Poor Pussy
All the guests sit in a circle, round the child chosen as 'pussy cat'. The cat approaches each guest in turn, on hands and knees, purring and saying 'Meow'.

Each player must stroke the cat's head three times saying 'Poor pussy'. The first player to laugh or smile is the next 'pussy cat'.

Sleeping Lions
All the guests lie on the floor. They must not move. You try to make them move by saying 'Susan, there is a wasp on your hair' or 'Look who's at the window', etc. If they move they are out. Those out can help try to make the others move too.

BLINDFOLD GAMES
Pin the Tail on the Donkey
- Draw a picture of a donkey without a tail. Mount it on a pinboard.
- Cut out a paper tail or make a woollen one and attach to a pin or piece of blue-tack.
- Blindfold one of the guests and lead him towards the donkey. Let him feel the board then spin him round three times and ask him to pin on the tail.
- Each player takes a turn and the winner is the one nearest to the correct position.
- You can either use the same tail and mark each spot with the player's initial, or make individual tails with each player's name on, so the donkey finally sprouts 15!

Traffic Lights
Divide all the children up into three groups; red, orange, and green. Blindfold them and get everybody to mingle together, and they have to join up with their group again, either by shouting out their colour until the group is complete, or, for a quieter version, by whispering it to one person at a time as they go round the room — you can penalize anyone who speaks too loudly by disqualifying their team. The first complete colour wins.

Squeak Piggy Squeak

Blindfold one player and give him a cushion. Turn him three times whilst the others sit down in a circle round him. The blindfolded player has to put the cushion on one of their laps and sit on it. He says 'Squeak piggy squeak' and the other player must squeak like a pig. If he guesses whose lap he is on, the second player is blindfolded.

NOTE: Remember to change places each time a new player is blindfolded.

Cat and Mouse

Ask the guests to form a circle. One is blindfolded and asked to stand in the middle. He is the cat. Another is chosen to be the mouse and he also stands in the middle. The cat has to catch the mouse. If he stands still and calls 'Meow' the mouse must squeak in reply. When the mouse is caught he becomes the cat and a new mouse is chosen.

Tasting Game

Put pieces of food – apple, mayonnaise, pickle, cheese – on a tray. Blindfold players and ask them to taste each item and say (or write down if they are older) what it is.

HUNTING GAMES

Treasure Hunt

A great favourite. Treasure hunts are wonderful outside but they can be played indoors too. You can make them more difficult as children get older.

EASY

- Tear up large pieces of coloured paper – one colour for each child – and hide them in easy-to-find places. When each child collects all the pieces he gets a prize.

MEDIUM
● Divide children into teams and draw simple clues on the coloured pieces, e.g. a picture of a tree or a table to show that is where the next clue is.

HARD
● Write words instead of the clues.

VERY HARD
● Make the clues into riddles, e.g. 'You'll find me . . . . on the edge in something long and green' (i.e. the next clue is hidden in long grass at the side of the garden).

Treasure
Adapt the treasure to the game. Gold coins (pirate party), feathers and arrows (cowboys and Indians), spider rubbers and animal chocolate bars (Animal Party); make sure there is something for every member of the team. You can also add little sweets on the way to keep the 'hunter' going.

Forfeits
If the children are older you could have one hoard of forfeit treasure – old potatoes, socks, etc. – but then give consolation prizes to keep everyone happy!

NOTE: If you have two teams, start at opposite ends of house/garden with clues in reverse order on different coloured paper.

Torn Pictures
A simple hunt when you are given half a picture and have to find the missing half. You can use birthday or Christmas cards or pictures torn from magazines.

EASY
● Hide the pictures around the house or put them all in a container and see how many each player or

pair can match up in 30 seconds or one minute.

MEDIUM
● Get the children to write down the name of the
  item.

HARD
● Choose photos shot from different angles so they
  are difficult to identify.

Tiny Hunt
A garden game. Give each child an old matchbox or
a tiny cardboard box (save from toy cars, old
jewellery, etc.). Ask them to collect as many items as
possible to fit in it.

The winner is the person who picks up the most.
You can play this game in pairs or groups of three
or four.

Hunt the Slipper
All the guests sit in a circle with one in the middle
who holds the slipper. He gives it to one of the
circle, shuts his eyes and says:
  'Cobbler, cobbler, mend my shoe
  Have it done by half past two
  Cobbler, cobbler tell me true
  Which of you has got my shoe?'
The others pass the slipper behind their backs and
stop as the rhyme ends. The guest in the middle has
to guess who has the slipper. If he is correct he
changes places with that player. If not, he repeats
the rhyme and has another go.

Chain Tag
In this race one player 'hunts' the rest. As he catches
them they form a chain until eventually everyone is
chasing the last player to be caught! As the chain
gets longer, it obviously gets slower.

Shipwreck

A garden game – unless you have a truly enormous playroom where children can jump on everything. Make sure that there is an assortment of objects and areas that children can jump on – for example a wooden bench, large mat, swing. All the children walk around in a circle until you call out "Shipwreck – oak tree!", whereupon they all race to touch the oak tree, and the last one there is out. The game continues until there are just two children left, and the winner then calls "Shipwreck" for the next go.

Sardines

One person hides whilst all the rest count to 50. They go off in different directions to find him or her and as each one does they hide in the same place. Eventually one player is left looking for the others who are all squashed!

Wool gathering (a)

Scatter short pieces of wool in house and/or garden. Give each child one colour. On the word 'Go' they have to find and tie together all pieces of appropriate colour. The winner is the child with the longest piece of wool.

Wool gathering (b)

Unravel one ball of wool per child. At the end tie a small present. Tangle the strands of wool round furniture and with each other. Give each child an end and on the word 'Go' they have to find their present.

FOLLOW THE ORDERS

Simon Says

The children face one leader (if they are young that will be an adult). The leader calls out certain actions and says 'Simon says . . . . lift one leg, scratch your tummy, waggle your ears' or whatever he is doing. All the children follow, but if the leader tells the others to do something without first saying 'Simon says' they must ignore him. Anyone who obeys the command is out. Use the birthday child's name instead of Simon.

Red, Orange, Green
This traffic lights game uses the red, orange and green as commands for 'as fast as you can', 'very slowly' and 'stop'. Have one person calling the colours as the guests walk, dance, act, or whatever.

On and Off
This is a confusing game as the players have to do the opposite!

Spread a blanket on the floor. When you call 'On the blanket' the children must get off it and vice versa. Anyone who makes a mistake is out.

Ship Ahoy
Fill a paddling pool and get the 'pirates' to *walk* round it (running can cause accidents). Shout 'Ship Ahoy' and the children all have to jump in. The last child into the pool is out each time.

GAMES FOR OLDER CHILDREN
See Disco, Pyjama, Dinner Party

Charades
Choose easy words ('sunshine', 'carpark', 'breakfast', 'drawer' (draw-her), 'Batman') which can be acted in separate syllables. Do one mime for the first syllable, one for the second and a third to show the whole thing.

John Brown's Body
Dim the lights and tell a creepy murder story (change the name to suit the ghostly tale!).

You are the murderer and you pass round bits of the body, e.g. grapes for eyes, sausage for fingers, a wig for hair, white sticks for bones, etc.

Do not terrify the children! If anyone is really scared take them out and get another adult to let them into the secret.

Murder in the Dark
Put a piece of paper, one for each player, in a hat. Mark one with a cross. Whoever draws it is the murderer. Dim the lights. The murderer must kill a victim by squeezing his shoulder. The victim screams and the lights go on. Everyone must stand still and try to keep a straight face. The other guests have to work out who is the murderer. Everyone must tell the truth *except* the murderer. The game continues until he or she has killed everyone!

NOTE: You can play a less scary version in daylight. The murderer winks at his victim.

Adverbs
One guest goes out of the room while the others choose an adverb – happily, noisily, crossly.

The guest returns and asks everyone to do something in this way, e.g. shake someone's hand, brush their hair, etc. When he guesses the adverb the player who was miming at the time goes out for the next turn.

Guess the Part of the Body
Blindfold one player and lead him into the room. Get him to feel the hair/leg/hand of each guest and see how many guests he can identify correctly.

I went to Peru and in my case I put . . .

An old favourite memory test game in which each person in turn says "I went to Peru and in my case I put" a certain object. The next person has to remember to pack that object, and adds another. You will be surprised how long the list becomes.

The Vicar's Cat

Sit in a circle and start at the beginning of the alphabet. One player says 'The Vicar's cat is an *angry* cat!' The next player has to use an adjective beginning with 'B' (leave out letter 'X'). If anyone cannot think of a word they are out.

Fizzbuzz

An old favourite counting game in which you have to say fizz for three or any number divisible by three, and buzz for five or any number divisible by five. So one to ten is one, two, fizz, four, buzz, fizz, seven, eight, fizz, buzz. By the way, 15 is fizzbuzz! Try to keep the pace up as the party shouts numbers around the room.

Twenty Items

Draw or write down 20 items beginning with a certain letter or number linked to your theme e.g. a particular colour . . . . . . animal, food, etc.

Consequences

Give everyone a piece of paper and pencil. Ask them to write down a girl's name followed by 'and'. Fold the paper and pass it on. Everyone writes down a boy's name and 'at'. Fold again then think of as funny a place as possible. Continue with 'he said', 'she said' and 'the consequence was'.

Everyone passes on for the last time then reads out their story. They are often very funny!

Picture Consequences
As above but players draw a head, a body and legs. They unfold the papers to reveal a wonderful hotchpotch of characters!

Hangman
Divide guests into teams. Give each team paper and pencils. One player from each team is the hangman. He has to think of a name, place, historical event and writes a dash for each letter. He tells the other players what type of word it is. They have to call out letters of the alphabet. If the letters are in the word, the 'hangman' fills them in.

If they are not he starts to draw the base of the gallows.

The aim is to find the word before he has drawn the gallows and the hanged man.

(Divide gallows into base, upright, crossbar, rope and then on to head, trunk, two arms and two legs.)

Memory Game
Put 20 objects on a tray. Bring it into the room and let the guests look at it for 30 seconds.

They must then jot down all the items – and the tray.

NOTE: With smaller children use fewer items and ask them to draw or speak them.

Pillowcase Game
Stuff a pillowcase with ten or 20 items – a sock, safety pin, pencil, toothbrush, carrot, etc.

Get the guests to feel the pillowcase and write down as many items they can identify as possible.

Draw the Missing Half
Provide half a torn picture stuck on a large sheet of

paper for each child. Get the children to complete the picture. The best drawing wins.

Blindfold Drawing
Blindfold all the guests and ask them to draw a scene. Keep adding details, e.g. a boat, the sea, a lighthouse, a swimmer, the beach, an ice-cream man. The funniest drawing is the winner.

The Journey Game
Write out some parts of the house on separate pieces of paper, one for each child. Tell them they all have one destination (say, a tree in the garden) and their journey must be via a certain point, where they will have to tick their name on a sheet listing all the guests. Then they are given their piece of paper with a starting point for the journey. You can add in stopover points as much as you like to keep them running about.

MISCELLANEOUS GAMES

Dressing up Game
Provide dresses, cloaks, masks, hats, make-up and mirrors. Let the children dress up. If they are older you could ask them to dress up as individual characters (nursery rhyme, historical, etc.) and then get them to 'act' who they are so that the others can guess.

Animals
Write the names of animals clearly on pieces of card, and tape one piece of card on the back of every guest. Then just ask your guests to help each other find out what their animal is, by reading each other's cards and acting out the animal, making the appropriate noises. A variation of this is for each guest to read their card and then hide it, so that they

themselves act out their animal. You will have cunningly arranged for there to be pairs of animals, and everyone has to find their other half!

Throw the Coin

Give each player six coins. Get them to stand in a circle around a plate. See who can throw most coins onto the plate.

Guess the Shout/Laugh/Snort

Divide players into two teams. One team is blindfolded. One by one they listen to the other team shouting/laughing/snorting. They have to write down or say who made the first, second, third shout, etc. The team with the most correct answers wins.

The Flour Game

This is a messy one. Make a pile of flour and put a chocolate on top of it. Each player in turn must make a cut with a knife into the flour pile – but if the chocolate moves, they have to eat it. That sounds fine you may say, but before they are allowed to touch it, tell them they can only touch the chocolate with their mouth! They will get covered in sticky flour! It is a good idea if players wear aprons for this one.

NOTE: This is a small selection of games. See *Children's Party Games* also in the Family Matters series for lots more ideas!

PARTY FOOD

PRELIMINARIES

What kind of food?

1 What age range are you catering for? Tinies love simple bite-sized food; older children are usually more adventurous.
2 Have you a colour or theme to follow? Much of the food and drink could be linked to your idea.
3 What is the season? Hot summer days, cold winter evenings, Christmas or Easter festivities?

WATCHPOINT: Are there children with allergies to be considered? Any vegetarians? Adequate choices need to be offered.

How much to serve?

This varies according to age, of course, but a rough guide is to allow for each individual:

- 4–6 savouries
- 3–4 small sweet items
- special pudding
- birthday cake
- 2–3 cold drinks

USEFUL QUANTITIES

An 850ml bottle of fruit drink yields 20–24 diluted drinks.

An average large sliced loaf, each sandwich round cut into quarters, yields about 44 sandwiches.

110g (4½oz) butter is required to spread thinly over one sliced loaf.

ADVANCE PLANNING

Start to prepare long before the party date. You will then enjoy yourself on THE DAY and the birthday child can have plenty of attention too!

Shopping

Make a list of all that needs to be bought. Spread your purchases out to help spread the cost! The following could be bought well in advance:

- bags of small frozen sausages
- frozen puff pastry
- ice cream
- ice cream cornets and wafers
- sweets for decorations, e.g. smarties, licorice allsorts etc
- paper cases
- packets of biscuits (including those needed for decoration)
- non-edible decorations for birthday cake
- props needed to produce cake, e.g. cocktail sticks, special food colourings, cake-board, candles
- crisps etc
- drinks such as squashes, lemonade, cola

Cooking

Pace the workload carefully and there'll be no last-minute panics. The following items could all be made successfully in advance:

- cheese straws (freezer or airtight container)
- cheese and marmite twists (airtight container)
- meringues (airtight container)
- large sponge slab (freezer) for birthday cake base
- small sponge buns (freezer)
- homemade biscuits (airtight container)
- homemade ice cream (freezer)
- supper dishes, e.g. pizza, burgers (freezer)

HANDY HINT
Don't forget to note what needs to be
removed from the freezer to defrost in time
for the party!

FINAL PREPARATIONS
Points on presentation
1 Small, neat items of food minimize waste and
   mess.
2 Finger food means no cutlery!
3 Decorated party tableware can be very expensive
   – consider buying plain white paper cups and
   plates, and adding your own motif (e.g. skull and
   crossbones, cowboy hat, birthday child's name etc.
4 Take clues from your theme – use silver foil
   containers to serve your space food; have a check
   tablecloth for your cowboy spread, etc.
5 An outdoor party tea could be packed into
   individual picnic boxes.
6 Arrange a variety of savouries on serving plates
   (and mix the cake and sweet items together in the
   same way). Each child then has all choices
   immediately at hand.
7 Make the table as colourful as possible – flowers,
   balloons, garnishes of tomato, carrots or fruit on
   serving dishes etc.
8 Let your child make and decorate place-cards or
   pipe names onto biscuits.

When to serve what
1 Plan to set the table with savouries before the
   party begins.
2 Introduce cakes when savoury interest begins to
   wane.
3 Ice cream could be served at tea-end, or later

when a refreshment break is needed between
games.
4 Display the birthday cake for all to see . . . but
possibly save the ceremony for a later break.

SANDWICHES
Preliminaries
Presentation is all important and not difficult. Think
about:

- varying bread colour
- *using playdough/pastry cutters to make shaped
  sandwiches (these could be linked to your theme;
  stars and moons for Halloween, animals for
  animal party etc.)
- colourful garnishes (slices of tomato, cucumber,
  carrot, radish flowers etc.)
- colourful fillings (see ideas below)
- small, neat shapes

TIP*
Use a small cutter to avoid too much
wastage per sandwich round.

Ideas for fillings
1 Tuna mixed with mayonnaise
2 Hard-boiled egg mashed and mixed with a little
  grated cheese, mayonnaise, mustard and cress
3 Tinned salmon mixed with lemon juice and a little
  tomato puree
4 Banana mashed and mixed with peanut butter
5 Finely grated red cheese, mixed with a little milk
  and tomato puree
6 Cooked ham, finely minced and moistened with a
  little mayonnaise

HANDY HINT
Younger children will probably prefer simpler fillings like marmite, egg, honey, etc.

SANDWICH PROJECTS

COTTAGE
- 5 rounds of sandwiches, with crusts removed
- Twiglets
- Carrot shapes and other salad items
- A little cream cheese

Cut two rounds into six oblong shapes, placing them as two layers on a board to make a single oblong. Cut remaining three rounds into 12 triangles. Use eight to form a roof and the rest a garden fence. Use pieces of carrot for a door and windows (attach with dabs of cream cheese), twiglets to form thatch for the roof, and fill the garden with parsley, celery, radish flowers, cherry tomatoes, etc.

TIP
Placing bread in freezer for 2 hours beforehand makes for easier handling!

CHESSBOARD
- 8 slices of brown and 8 slices of white bread
- Fillings

Make eight rounds of sandwiches, using one white and one brown slice for each round. Remove crusts, and cut each sandwich into four squares. Then arrange on a board in two layers alternating the colours. Use several fillings for an element of surprise!

PARTY CAKES

The centrepiece of the occasion, it is worth spending time and thought on the cake you choose to make.

Preliminaries

- Don't leave the party cake to the last minute – rushing may lead to disaster!
- Sponge cake should be cooked a day or two in advance so that it is easier to ice and cut. (NB sponge freezes well).
- The simplest cakes can be just as effective as the more complicated (see ideas below!) so choose carefully.
- Choice? Match the cake to your theme; try something seasonal, or simply let your child choose!

Equipment

1 Food colourings
2 Paint brushes
3 Icing bags and nozzles
4 Greaseproof paper
5 Cocktail sticks
6 Smarties, licorice allsorts, hundreds and thousands

HANDY HINT
Keep a box of licorice allsorts in your cupboard and you'll be ready for that emergency cake!

Basic Mixtures

SPONGE
- 100g (4oz) soft margarine
- 100g (4oz) caster sugar

- 2 eggs
- 100g (4oz) self-raising flour
- 1 level tsp baking powder

Beat ingredients together well and pour into a well-greased tin (or tins) and bake at 180°C (350°F), Gas Mark 4 for about 30 minutes.

BUTTER ICING
- 175g (6oz) butter or soft margarine
- 250g (9oz) sieved icing sugar

Allow the fat to soften and beat in the sieved sugar until fluffy and pale.

GLACÉ ICING
- 225g (8oz) icing sugar
- 2 tbls water

Sieve the sugar twice to make it really fine. Add the water gradually until the icing is of the right consistency to coat the back of a wooden spoon.

HANDY HINT
Bought fondant paste provides an easy instant cake covering. Knead in colour where required.

EASY CAKES TO ASSEMBLE
The following cake ideas are grouped according to original shape. Each idea is briefly described and is offered to you as a starting point for your own individual interpretation!

Swiss Roll Shape

TANK ENGINE
Cut away a small top section from one end of your

swiss roll (somewhere for the driver to stand!). Cover the roll in smooth chocolate butter icing, and ice in details as wished. Add a piece of mini roll for a chimney; biscuits for wheels; licorice allsorts for buffers. Make trucks from chocolate mini rolls, cutting the tops away so that they can be filled with sweets. Decorate with smarties and add more allsorts for wheels. Use cocktail sticks to join your trucks to the engine and set the whole assembly on a licorice railway line!

SPACE ROCKET

Ice the roll with butter icing and stand on one end. Support it with 4 chocolate finger biscuits stuck in at angles (foil wrapped ones look nice). Make a cone out of thin card for the nose. Complete decoration to individual taste.

SAUSAGE DOG

Ice the roll with chocolate butter icing, adding pieces of chocolate fingers for legs and tail; a chocolate mini roll (secured with a cocktail stick) for the head and use licorice allsorts to make ears, eyes and the nose.

CRACKERJACK!

Cut your swiss roll in half. Make 2 cardboard cylinders about 7cm (3in) long, and fit onto the end of each swiss roll half. Cover the 2 halves with butter icing (extending over the card). Fill the halves with foil-covered chocolate money (or sweets), push together and ice over the crack. Pull apart to serve!

Pudding Basin Shape
(Use a 3 egg quantity of sponge for a 1.2 litre (2pt) basin. Cook for 55–60 minutes at 160°C (325°F) Gas Mark 3.)

HALLOWEEN CAKE
Colour 350g (12oz) fondant paste with blue colouring, and roll out thinly to cover the cake. Paint the cake with a little apricot glaze and mould paste to the sponge, cutting away excess fondant. Model a simple cat shape from the excess, paint with black food colour and leave to dry. Roll out a little marzipan and use cutters to make moons and stars. Attach these to the cake with a little jam. Position the cat on the top! More ingenious modellers can also make black spiders or orange pumpkins.

WHITE MOUSE
Cover the cake thickly with butter icing, forking it well all over the icing for fur, then add pink marshmallows for ears and nose; small licorice rounds for eyes and pieces of white pipecleaner for whiskers!

HEDGEHOG
Cover the cake with chocolate butter icing, forking well forward at one end to form the head. Use cherries for eyes and a piece of licorice roll for the snout. Choose pieces of chocolate sticks (e.g. Matchmakers) to cover the body for spines.

LADYBIRD
Cover the cake with red butter icing. Shape a sponge bun to form the head, cover with chocolate icing and attach to body. Use cherries for eyes and angelica or chocolate sticks for antennae. Gently mark in wing division on the body with the end of a knife, and arrange brown smarties over the top for the spots!

SOCCER BALL

Make 2 basin cakes. Sandwich together with butter icing and then shape into a round, flattening the underside slightly for stability! Cover cake with uncoloured butter icing. Mark in hexagonal shapes with a skewer dipped in cocoa. Make eyelet rounds and laces with licorice. Place the ball on green-tinted coconut for grass!

WIGWAM

Trim sides of the cake a little, placing trimmed pieces on the top to give a better shape. Colour 350g (12oz) fondant paste yellow and drape around the cake, pulling one lower edge back slightly to simulate the tent opening. Crimp the top edges and insert pieces of chocolate finger biscuits for poles. Decorate with little shapes cut from coloured fondant, or smarties etc.

RABBIT

Make 2 basin cakes. Trim one to make the head and attach to the body with a little butter icing. Similarly attach a small sponge bun to the body for the tail. Cover the cakes with icing and press on coconut. Form ears from marzipan and attach using cocktail sticks. Add smarties for eyes and nose, and tie a pretty ribbon around the neck. Make use of coconut grass once more!

CHARLIE CLOWN

Make 2 basin cakes. Trim one to make the head, saving 2 pieces for ears. Fold 2 lengths of coloured paper as if to make fans, then paste together to make a ruffle. Using icing attach ears and ruffle to body, then head to ruffle. Cover head and ears with uncoloured butter icing and body with chocolate icing. Decorate body with smarties and silver balls etc. Make facial features with licorice and cherries. Colour some coconut orange and sprinkle over the ears. Use strips of licorice for hair and place a foil party hat on top!

CINDERELLA

Gently push a Sindy doll into your cake, feet first, so just her torso remains outside. Cover the cake with butter icing. Halve pink and white marshmallows and press into the 'skirt' for a pretty design. Using 30 cm (1 ft) of ribbon, start winding around the doll's body to represent a bodice, tying the ends in a large bow at the waist. Add other decorations to taste – sugar flowers etc.

TIP
Dip scissors into water before cutting marshmallows and they'll cut easily!

TOADSTOOL HOME

Using a 4-egg mix make up 1 × 1.2 litre (2pt) basin cake and 1 cylinder cake, using a clean 793g (1lb 12oz) can. Cover the cylinder with butter icing. Brush basin cake with apricot glaze and cover with red fondant, pulling edges in underneath. Put cakes together. Use licorice allsorts for a chimney, windows and door (pipe in window panes and knobs). Finely slice an allsort for toadstool spots. Make a garden with green coconut, sugar flowers etc.

Round Shape

BASKET CAKE

Bake a 3-egg sponge mixture in 2 × 20cm (8in) tins. Cut the centre out of one of the cake. Use chocolate butter icing to sandwich the cakes together, then cover the top and sides with further icing (not the central well). Use white glacé icing to pipe basket-weave on the sides. Make a handle from thin card, covering it with pretty paper or ribbon and attach to the sides of the cake (secure with cocktail sticks if necessary, though don't attempt to lift the cake with it). Decorate and fill the basket with sweets, marzipan fruits, Easter eggs and chicks.

BUTTERFLY

Bake a 3-egg sponge mixture in 2 × 20cm (8in) tins. Sandwich cakes together with butter icing. Cut the cake in half and reverse so that the 2 curved sides are back to back. Cut small triangular pieces from the centre of each curved side to make the head (diamond shape). Ice the cake with coloured glacé icing, and pipe a pretty design with icing of a contrasting colour. Use Matchmaker sticks for antennae and silver balls for eyes to complete this cake.

SWIMMING POOL

Use 1 deep 20cm (8in) tin for your cake this time. Cut a layer out of the cake-top (leaving a narrow wall around the edge). Cover the sides and edge of the cake with chocolate butter icing. Arrange chocolate fingers in an upright position all around the cake. Mash up a quantity of green jelly and fill the pool! Make a ladder for the side from licorice and Matchmaker sticks. Use further sticks fixed with a little icing to make lilos. Add a cocktail umbrella and a small doll or two.

PIRATE

Use 1 deep 20cm (8in) tin for your cake. Trim the top edge to the shape of a pirate's hat. Cover the hat section with yellow butter icing and the face with uncoloured butter icing. Cut out a skull and crossbones from black paper and position on the hat. Use jelly beans and licorice for his features – a halved chocolate biscuit makes an eye patch with a licorice strap. (Heap some chocolate money around the board!)

RACING-TRACK

Use 1 20cm (8in) ring tin for this cake. Cut the cake in half horizontally, then shave a small piece from one end of each circle to enable the figure-of-eight to make a snug fit. Cover the cakes with chocolate butter icing. Cut 2 strips of cardboard 15 × 6cm (6 × 2½in). Position one as a flyover bridge and the other as a ramp running off the cake. Cover them with more icing. Position pieces of Matchmaker sticks around the edges of the track. Use a red lollipop for a stop sign. Make a chequered flag and position this and some toy racing cars on the cake to complete.

RECORD
Cover with chocolate butter icing. Press sugar strands onto sides and mark grooves on the top with a fork. A centre of white glacé icing and a few musical notes cut in licorice to finish.

COLOUR CAKE
Keep icing and decorations different shades of a single colour.

CHARACTERS
Cover the cake with fondant paste and leave for a day or two to dry out. Trace a favourite cartoon character (Batman, Disney, Thundercats, My Little Pony etc.) or faces of cowboys and Indians onto greaseproof paper. Secure to top of cake with pins (colour-headed for safety) and lightly prick design through. Use food colouring pens (available from cake specialist shops) to outline and fill in designs.

Square, Rectangular, or Loaf Shape

PIANO
Use a rectangular cake. Cut a section off the short end. Stand the larger piece on its end and position the smaller section against it. Cover with chocolate butter icing. Place tablets of white chocolate along the keyboard edge and use small pieces of licorice to make the black keys. A slice of ice cream wafer makes a neat ledge to hold a little book of music!

PAINT BOX

Use a rectangular cake. Cut one groove across the centre of the cake (large enough to take a paint brush) and cut a small well across one end (to form water container). Cover the cake with coffee-flavoured butter icing. Position chocolate Match-makers around the top edges of the cake and press chocolate sugar strands against all the sides. Position the paintbrush in its place and line with more Matchmakers. Fill the reservoir with blue butter icing, and position winegums to represent the paints.

CHRISTMAS TREE

Make 2 sponge cakes in swiss roll tins (4-egg mixture total). Sandwich together with butter icing, then cut to a simple tree shape. Attach 2 cut-out pieces to the top, and stick 2 others together to form a tub. Cover the tree with green butter icing and fork up. Use red icing for the tub. Decorate with silver balls, smarties etc . . . don't forget a star for the top!

TREASURE CHEST

Use a small rectangular cake and a cake baked in a swiss roll tin. Trim the shallow cake to make a lid for the chest. Cut a layer out of the base cake (leaving a narrow ledge around the top). Cover the sides and edges of the base with chocolate butter icing. Ice the underside of the lid and position on chest (use cocktail sticks to secure at the back, and pieces of rock to prop at the front). Ice the top of the lid, and decorate the chest. Fill with foil-covered money and/or chocolate buttons (the ones covered with hundreds and thousands are effective).

WINDING DOWN

Parties go in peaks and troughs; the excitement builds up to tea-time then quietens down again before a second bout of activity games.

Try to avoid a situation where parents arrive to collect screaming, over-excited children. Stop the mad dash round the garden, Murder in the Dark or balloon bursting, ten minutes before the end and gather the children round.

Watch out for anyone who has not won a prize.

Have a few spares and award prizes to 'All girls in blue dresses', 'All boys with red shirts', or whatever the losers happen to be wearing!

Depending on the age of the children have a few winding down suggestions.

Picture Consequences; Blindfold Drawing; ordinary picture drawing (for younger children); Sleeping Lions (always very popular); animal story; let younger children ride in the garden, i.e. 'sit and ride' toys, matchbox hunt.

Avoid playing a nail-biting game like Pass the Parcel or Treasure Hunt at the end or the guests will not want to leave.

If you finish a few minutes early you could put on a video tape but parents may have trouble dragging children away in the midst of *Mary Poppins* so choose something short. If you have made a video of the party, allocate the last 15 minutes to showing it. They'll want it run through at least three times to laugh at themselves!

Have party bags ready. While the last games are being played you can cut the cake if it was not eaten at tea-time and put pieces in the bags.

Do not have the children waiting by the door with

coats on; some parents may be a few minutes late and nothing will make them feel more guilty! Get one adult to keep the quieter activities going while another answers the doorbell quickly and fetches coats.

. **NOTE:** If you have asked the children to bring extra equipment, e.g. wellington boots, aprons or toys, put these in labelled bags ready to give to the appropriate parent.

Some hosts like to invite other parents in for a drink but you need plenty of adult help to do this. Also the children who have behaved perfectly all afternoon often become ratty and irritable when their parents arrive!

On the whole it is probably better to save adult entertaining for another occasion.

One final word

The most important key to success is for everyone to have fun. If you enjoy going to town on cooking and decorations, that's fine, but do not try to compete with other parties where there have been designer costumes and decorations and a perfectly iced birthday cake. Children do not notice these things, or care.

They will remember birthdays for the rest of their lives for a fun atmosphere and excitement – not the texture of the fairycakes or the state of the sitting room carpet. The best birthday treat you can give your child is the memory of a warm, happy day full of laughter and merriment. Keep smiling, relax and you will enjoy the day too!

INDEX